I0187199

The Importance of Me: Advice from a Friend

Copyright © 2018 by Nicole Sherrill-Corry, Ph.D.

ISBN-13: 978-0692109670

ISBN-10: 0692109676

Library of Congress Cataloging – in – Publication Data

Printed in the United States of America

IMPORTANCE OF ME:

ADVICE FROM A FRIEND

Nicole Sherrill-Corry, Ph.D.

To my daughters, Treasure and Brooke, Honey Girls Amiyah and Brynn, and Cynthia Stoner. Thank you for helping me to be the best mother, daughter, friend, Honey and person that I can possibly be.

CONTENTS

THE IMPORTANCE OF ME

WHY AM I IMPORTANT?

God has richly blessed me. I'm in a second marriage, to a wonderful, supportive man. I have four smart, beautiful children and a circle of old and new friends who are always there for me. I have a PhD in Counseling Studies and run my business that has grown beyond my craziest dreams and positioned my family to live comfortably, wanting for nothing.

So, who am I to talk to you about your problems, doubts, and fears? Where do I get off acting as though I know what you're going through, as if I understand your pain, loneliness and heartache? How can I, you wonder, enjoy this amazing reality that God has spoken into being and still claim to be in a position to give you advice?

The reason is simple, my sister. I've been there. Where I am now is a far cry from whence I came. My current reality is an ocean away from the reality I once lived. I've experienced pain, neglect, sadness and betrayal. I've asked tough, soul-searching questions and shed plenty of tears. I've suffered through many dark nights while waiting for the sun to rise, unsure whether tomorrow would truly be a better day.

So, believe me, my friend, I do know what it feels like to hurt. But I also know what it feels like to overcome, to triumph and to find my true strength.

And that's why I'm in a position to help you by passing on my advice, from one friend to another, so you, too, can benefit from the difficult lessons I've learned.

I grew up in Salisbury, North Carolina, in several different places because we moved a lot. I mainly remember my grandparents' humble house in a public housing project on Linn Lane. Nobody there had a lot of money. It wasn't a bad place for a kid to grow up; there was a playground right across the way, and you could almost smell the oil heating at local famous chicken eatery nearby. They had the best fried chicken! Further down you could see the cemetery and beyond that, a park. When it was hot we happily fled the confines of our apartments and played outdoors, hoping for some nice cool breezes. Even then, though,

I had few friends and was never really sure whether anyone was in my corner.

I was the second child born to an unwed teenage mother. My father was a married man. My mom sang with the family band, and they toured from church to church on Sundays singing for the Lord.

There was no fanfare when I arrived. I was not a child who was longed for, prayed for or planned. I was the apple of no one's eye. Basically, when my mom had me it meant nothing more than another black, unwed teenage girl had given birth. I'm not knocking my mother as she was just a kid herself, but I received no nurturing, and nobody made me feel wanted.

Suffice it to say I was lost.

My mother had only a high-school diploma. I feel she constantly looked for love through her relationships yet seldom found it. Besides faithfully paying his court-ordered child support every month until I turned 18, my father had little to do with me.

Coincidentally, my father's wife was pregnant around the same time my mother carried me, so I am the same age as my half-brother.

I lived with my grandparents, my mother, my aunts and my brother, who was just a little older than me. A baby sister soon came along, and in time another brother followed. The home was cramped. Times were hard.

My grandfather worked at a nearby cotton mill, and my grandmother cleaned houses for white people in the more upscale part of town. Her clients weren't rich but lived much better than we did.

My grandmother was a hard, cheerful worker, and the people she cleaned for loved her. My grandfather's employers loved him, too. They knew the value of good, honest work, and weren't ashamed of doing manual labor. I still occasionally run into members from some of those old families, and they still speak highly of my grandparents after all these years.

Whatever we had, we supplemented it with food stamps. While we weren't hungry and hardly anything went to waste. I can't say I lacked for anything material. Well, maybe I longed for nicer clothes at times, but occasionally my mom or grandparents managed to take us shopping at good department stores.

While my grandparents showed me love as best they could, my mother was ambivalent toward me. She always sought love from others and was often disappointed. We grew up in the church, and soon my sister and I also began singing. It was part of the family tradition.

Life wasn't all bad, and we had some good times. I especially remember the sleepovers we had when I was about seven or eight. Most of them were with two other girls who remain among my best friends today. We had fun. We used to put on Sister Sledge concerts, with much attitude. It was adorable.

I'm certain my lack of interaction with my father negatively impacted some of the choices I made later in life. I didn't know what it felt like to be loved by a male, so I didn't know how to expect or demand respect from them, which left me feeling like I didn't belong anywhere. For a long time, I was drifting. My father never availed himself for the fatherly support I desperately craved, and I'm sure his indifference has impacted my relationships – particularly those with men.

I also grew up innocent, knowing very little about sex. Some kids are taught the birds and the bees by their mom or dad. They giggle and squirm and are glad when "the lesson" is over but at least they get that much. The closest thing I got to sex education was the day my mom asked my grandmother to take my sister and me to the health department for birth control classes. There we were, a group of girls ages eleven and twelve, listening to a lecture on something we couldn't comprehend.

The health department lecture didn't do me much good. I lost my virginity out of peer pressure when I was fifteen, to an older boy at a house party.

The girlfriend with whom I'd gone to the party had wandered off with a boy, leaving me alone. I barely understood what was going on.

When he reached for me, I knew on some level I had the power to say no. But why would I? I wanted so desperately to feel important and wanted. If I'd turned him down, I reasoned in my immature mind someone else would get the attention. So even though I know now it wasn't what was best for me, I went with him.

Losing your virginity is supposed to be special, a transition from girlhood to adulthood. Yet at that age, having sex for the first time left almost no impression on me. I didn't even know enough about life, or about sexual matters to feel guilty or ashamed. I also didn't judge myself, which I guess was a good thing.

Not long after my first sexual intercourse encounter, my mom sent my sister and me to Fort Lauderdale to spend the summer with our uncle. Naturally, as teenage girls, I was soon crushing on another cute guy. I started following him around and was happy about any attention he paid me.

We wound up lying down next to each other, just snuggling. Nothing else went on, but word got back to my uncle and he wasn't happy. Instead of yelling at me; however, that smart man sat me down for a talk I remember even today. He explained to me, very lovingly, how much I was worth. He told me I was valuable.

I was blown away! It was the first time in my life a man thought enough of me to explain that I was worth something. "I don't care what you do," he said, "but don't ever feel undervalued. Don't ever give yourself to someone who doesn't respect you."

That was something I really needed to hear. As far as I was concerned, I was a teenager now and was going to do whatever I wanted. There was no one around to curb me or guide me, and yet my uncle took the time to teach me otherwise. "Hey, you're going to do great things, but you need to believe it for yourself," he said. My uncle was the first person who helped me understand my importance. Despite my uncle's sage advice and concern for me, I got pregnant with my first baby when I was just a junior in high school. My son's father was a few years older than me and in the military. Even as a high school junior, I had very little supervision and came and went as I pleased. My mother had just gotten married to a man who didn't much care for us, so we did what we wanted.

The young man and I had been chatting on the phone for a couple of weeks. It was nothing huge, certainly not a great romance. He was someone for me to talk to.

One night we were at a party together and this cute older guy was looking at me like he wanted to eat me up. *I must be pretty*, I thought. *I must be okay.* I felt I was in love. Mistaking attention for love is easy to do when you have no idea what love really is – not to mention when there was so little of it floating around when you were growing up and you didn't have a daddy around to show you what real love feels and looks like. The reality is I just didn't know how to discern when a young man was acting the right way toward me versus just trying to get in my pants.

So, there he was paying attention to me. Sure, it was the wrong kind of attention, but it was attention nonetheless and I loved it. At some point during the night, we walked across the street to his friend's house. I was virtually just as ignorant as I was during my first time three years before and therefore can't say much about what it was like or how it felt. It just happened, and that was that.

After that night we talked on the phone, but there was never anything more to "us." He soon moved on, probably to someone more experienced who knew how to please him.

A few weeks later I started getting sick and didn't know why. My mom had been monitoring my cycle since I'd started having it two years before. My cycle came like clockwork, so mom always knew when I was due.

When it didn't come, she asked, "Is something wrong with you?"

"What do you mean is something wrong with me?" I responded. I didn't even realize what was going on, but mom did. She bought a home pregnancy test for me, and that's how we found out I was with child.

My mom was angry and disappointed, and there was some pressure put on me to have an abortion. I was just a kid and disagreeing with what she told me to do didn't even cross my mind. Mom even made an appointment for me at a clinic when I was just six or eight weeks along. But my aunt was very spiritual, and she decided to intervene to save the life of my unborn baby.

Instead of arguing on a philosophical level, my aunt chose a tactic that turned out to be very effective. On the morning of my appointment, she brought home anti-abortion brochures and pamphlets with graphic, horrifying photos of what happens to a fetus during an abortion and showed them to mom and me.

The photos got to me on deep and basic levels. I looked at them and knew I couldn't go through with the abortion and told mom I was going to keep my baby. She wasn't happy. She knew from experience how hard life as a teen mother would be. She also knew the impact another baby would have on the family. Even so, she didn't force me to have an abortion. She understood how I felt about it and respected my wishes, and I'm grateful for that.

Back in those days when an unmarried girl in the black community was pregnant, she had to go to church and confess her sin in front of the entire congregation, then ask for forgiveness. Just the girls, mind you, not the men or boys who were partly responsible for the pregnancies in the first place. That's the way things worked and still work. Women bear the burden of their sexuality alone, while men escape culpability as though babies generate spontaneously, born solely of the mother's sinful thoughts.

So, girls got dragged into church to stand with their heads lowered in shame as a group of scowling elders and frowning church-goers judged and ultimately "forgave" them. I'm sure there were numerous times when many men and boys sat among the congregation knowing full well the "sin" was half theirs, yet they remained silent, perfectly happy to let the girl or woman face the ridicule and take the fall.

I was never subjected to that ridiculous walk of shame because my outspoken grandmother questioned why I should have to be humiliated when other pregnant girls in the church who hadn't suffered through it. Nevertheless, after I started showing I got dirty, "you-should-be-ashamed-of-yourself" looks. I guess my pregnancy was extra shocking for everyone because from the outside looking in our family was just fine. The gossip mills churned overtime about me being knocked up. Hey, Salisbury is a small town, and I guess people didn't have anything better to do.

Despite being pregnant, I tried living a normal life. I continued going out and about, and I'm grateful my family didn't try to keep me inside as if they were ashamed of me.

A couple of the girls I typically hung with got banned from seeing me because their folks thought I would be a bad influence on them. It was okay, because being ostracized was nothing new to me.

Back then, pregnant girls were sent to a special school separate from the rest of the students. I guess the good thing about that is I was allowed to continue my education versus being kicked out of school altogether. I spent my junior year in the "special school."

My baby was breech, and after twenty-one intense hours of labor they decided to perform a C-section. I was just a young girl, scared out of my mind. I was in mad pain, and the baby's father was nowhere in sight. My mom was right by my side the entire time and was a huge comfort to me.

When I first laid eyes on my son and the nurse placed him in my arms, I was in awe. I absolutely could not believe I had brought a human being into the world. I was so happy! I honestly couldn't believe what I had achieved. I had a child!

My son's father was trifling and contributed nothing toward his expenses. I made do with the few items I had, most of them given to me at a small baby shower my family threw for me.

Six weeks after I had my son, I went back to school for just a short period. I was aggressive and got into several fights. The other kids were merciless, often picking at me for having gotten pregnant, and my philosophy was, *If you try to hurt me, I'm going to hurt you.*

I began dating another boy from around the block that I'd known for a few years. He was so popular that other girls competed fiercely for him. I fought them over him, too, and I think he liked that.

I ended up dropping out of school because I just didn't feel as though I belonged there anymore. My life had changed dramatically. I was now a mother and had a mouth to feed. When the Pampers and few items I'd received as gifts from the baby shower ran out, I started working as a cashier and cook at night to pay the bills.

I worked at the restaurant for six or seven months before quitting to re-focus on my education. This time I signed up for my adult high school diploma. I knew how much an education would be worth in the long run, so getting that piece of paper was important to me.

While I worked and studied, my mom and grandmother juggled taking care of my son with their jobs. Needless to say my carefree teenage life was over.

I picked up temporary jobs, here, there and everywhere. I did mostly clerical work, gathering experience along the way. Eventually I enrolled in a general education program at a community college, taking basic core subjects like English and math. My efforts were in preparation for enrolling in a degree program; however, I didn't finish and was there for only a short time.

By now I was spending more and more time with the cute high-schooler I used to fight over, who would eventually become my husband. He helped me with my son, and after graduating high school he started working as a sexton in the church. A year after I had my son, we had a daughter together.

Right now, you may be thinking, *Oh, that's wonderful! What a good man to step up to the plate!* Well, trust me when I tell you it wasn't nearly as glamorous or as good as it seemed. Our relationship was mired by abuse. We argued often, and as I bettered myself with education, he became more and more resentful of me. Instead of celebrating my success and recognizing that the more educated I was the better my chances of obtaining a good-paying job, he was resentful.

He was jealous, too, and got upset if I looked at another man or if someone even spoke to me. Given how good looking and popular he was, not to mention the fact that I and other women used to literally fight over him, I never understood his insecurities. Maybe he was tripping because we were not longer high-school kids with everything being handed to us. We were young adults out there in a tough world, and his ego was no longer getting constantly stroked like it did back in high school.

In terms of his outbursts, he didn't strike at once. Instead, he'd let things build up, as if he was thinking, *"You just wait…"* In his twisted mind he gave me free pass after free pass for whatever "crime" I'd committed. But he didn't forget them. When he exploded he punched and hit. Sometimes I tried to defend myself, as I knew a thing or two about fighting. But the average woman cannot beat the average man in a fight, and I was no exception. He hit me so hard one time I thought he'd broken my nose.

Twice before we were married I summoned the courage to go to the police. And twice I dropped the charges. I was afraid he'd leave me alone with the children, and he also begged and pleaded for me to drop the charges. He promised, as most men do, that he'd change. He went to counselling and took anger management classes and seemed sincere both times he went, always promising he'd never do it again. Each time I believed him.

I talked to my mother about the abuse and she was livid. From that point on she was turned against him and said, "He's got to go." At first, I didn't listen.

After a particularly severe beating sent me to the emergency room, I decided to leave. By that time, we'd had a second child together, a daughter, bringing to three the number of children I had. I took her with me to hide out with relatives in Florida, leaving my two older children, just toddlers at the time, with my mom and his mother.

When I returned my mother and I fell out, because once I was able to get my children back the benefits she was receiving for them dried up. She put us out, and we wound up in a homeless shelter for a week.

The shelter was a nightmare. We slept on little mats on the floor. Their father came with us, even though he had a clean, dry bed at his grandmother's house. It was all a big show, an attempt to prove to me that he was about being with and taking care of his family. It really was nothing more than his way of trying to woo me back.

I applied for public housing and got it, but it was chaotic and I hated it. It was apparent to me more now than ever that to live the lifestyle I wanted, the one I felt I was meant to live; I'd have to study hard and work even harder.

Newly single, I dated a little, though my ex was busy telling tales behind my back to sully my name. He even lied on me in conversations with my mother. Although he had relationships of his own, he was insanely jealous of any I tried to have and did everything he could to intervene and mess things up for me.

Eventually, somehow, he convinced me he'd try to be the man I needed him to be. So, one more time, I took him back. Needless to say, the cheating continued, as did the verbal and emotional abuse. I was like a hamster on a wheel, running and running but going nowhere fast.

I couldn't believe I was taking that from him, but I did. I knew it was wrong, but for some reason I stayed with him. Again, and again, he promised things would get better and they did – for a while. Despite the beatings I married him because I thought I was in love. Now, I know I was more in love with the idea of my kids having a family – the kind of family I never had.

Once we married he stopped using his fists against me, but there were other forms of abuse. He refused to pay bills, so I ended up shouldering most of the financial burden of our household. Two months after our wedding I found out I was pregnant again.

As you may have guessed, eventually the physical abuse resumed. He started beating me again about two years into the marriage. Like so many women trapped in bad marriages, I left and promised myself this time it was for good. Then he wooed me back again. I was working on my bachelor's degree and relying on my mother and mother-in-law to care for my kids. I knew deep down this wasn't the best life they could be living, so desperate for them to have a stable life I returned to him. After earning my bachelor's degree, I earned my master's degree, joined a sorority and began to have a social life. The more my life expanded, the more I realized I was out growing my husband. I had friends, an education, a good job and a promising future. By comparison, he was a janitor. I'm not putting him down because at least it was a legal job. My problem with him – despite the abuse and his philandering ways, of course – was he lacked ambition and seemed content with his low-paying, menial job.

Despite his foundering, I stayed focused, enrolled in a Ph.D. program and began lecturing. Everything opened up for me financially. I started doing consultant work, was holding down three jobs, going to school and being a mother to my children. It was extremely exhausting, but I had a clear picture in my head about who I was going to be and what I wanted – and didn't want – out of life. I didn't want to live on welfare, and I made up my mind I was never going to go there again.

I knew my husband was still cheating on me. He should have been ashamed to even think about going outside the marriage given the mess I'd put up with from him for years, but I guess that meant nothing to him. As time wore on, he and our marriage meant less and less to me. I started planning my exit from him.

The kids knew what was going on, and I worried about the effect it was having on them. My youngest child, though just under five, was particularly in tune to the situation. You know how sensitive kids can be sometimes. Well, one day when I was feeling especially down, he somersaulted into the room, threw his arms around me and said, "Even if nobody else loves you, I love you." It's a line from Al Green's song, *I'm So in Love with You.* It almost broke my heart. In that very moment I decided to leave my no count husband for good.

I proceeded carefully but meticulously. I began by saving money and looking at houses on the sly. I gave him fair warning, with a three-month ultimatum. I told him to shape up or I was shipping out. I wondered how he would take it, but he didn't seem to care, saying "Whatever." Deep down he probably cared, because after all I was his meal ticket. He probably just didn't believe me when I told him.

I know the violence is worst for most women when they try to leave their abusive husbands or boyfriends, but I wasn't afraid. I'd studied the situation and done a lot of reading. I was smarter and better educated than before, and I knew he couldn't get in my head anymore.

In March 2007, I moved out.

ADVICE FROM A FRIEND

Girlfriend, I hear you. You have your challenges, and I have mine. Yet having gone through what I did, not to mention watching other women fall and get up again, I feel compelled to share what I've learned.

Do you know what it feels like to wish there was someone, perhaps a friend, who would share a pot of coffee with you and listen to your problems? Have you ever wished for a friend who would listen without judging and draw upon her experiences and knowledge to give you advice?

Today, I am that friend for you. And contained within these pages is the best advice I can offer.

Women are faced with so many challenges in life. We struggle with being wives, mothers, workers and friends. We also struggle with our own internal battles. Likewise, our responsibilities change with each phase of our lives. What we need to overcome as students is different than what we face in the workplace. The demands of being employees differ from those of being employers. The responsibilities of being parents are different from those of caring for our elderly parents.

Making things more difficult, these responsibilities and challenges are all intertwined. We can't stop being moms just to handle problems at work. At times our families and our communities require our attention simultaneously, requiring creativity to manage the conflicts.

It takes determination and perseverance to equip ourselves with the tools we need to meet life's demands. And doing so is a long-term learning process as opposed to a one-shot deal. The good news is as we overcome life's challenges we experience growth that equips us for the next set of challenges we'll face. It's sort of like the adage, "That which doesn't kill us makes us stronger." Believe me. There's a lot of truth in that.

Each day is different and has its own issues and circumstances. As we go through our days we'll be faced with negative and positive experiences. How we choose to react to those experiences says a lot about us.

With everything I've been through in my life, including the good, the bad and the ugly, I've found ultimate happiness that moves us forward each day is every woman's dream. Ultimate happiness to me is knowing I am doing what I want, where I want with whom I want.

Doing what you want ensures you remain true to yourself and to others. I don't know about you, but I sleep better at night knowing I've accomplished the goals I set for myself, my clients, my husband, my children and my friends. I love the happiness I feel after checking items off my to-do list.

I also like knowing everything I do is from the heart. Okay. I know that sounds a little corny. But think about how you handle your duties and face your obstacles. Don't you find things easier to manage when you operate from a position of love? I'm not talking solely about love for the people involved but also love for the task itself. Love for the fact that you're in a position to share your knowledge and expertise with those who need it. Most importantly, do it out of love for yourself. We learn by doing, and we grow by serving.

We also grow by taking on life's challenges to ensure we're able to grow and move to where we want to be. We must press on without thinking or worrying about upsets that come along the way. Simply put. We must do what has to be done.

It helps, of course, to have strong support from family and friends. The difficulty – not to mention the hurt and pain – comes when those you expect to have your back step away from you or try to pull you down for whatever reasons.

FRIENDSHIP AND ADVICE

Friendship, perseverance and faith are very important, especially when things aren't going as they should be. Looking through the lens of other people may shine light on some of the problems they're having while helping you understand some of the barriers affecting you as a woman.

We live in such an egocentric world that it's easy to be fooled into thinking our point of view is the only one – or at least the only one that matters. But often the opinions, perspectives and vision of others helps bring clarity to our own dilemmas. The reason for that is simple: What we encounter on our life's journey – including the people we meet, the troubles we face, our joys and sorrows and our successes and failures – affect how we see the world. And I don't mean only the narrow, tiny corner of the world we occupy.

Being in tune with others' thoughts, views and perspectives allows us to comment with loving-kindness on what we see happening in the lives of others. When we all get outside of ourselves and practice understanding situations from others' points of view, the world becomes a better place. Now, you may be saying, "Hold on. I'm a strong, independent woman. Why do I need others telling me what to do? Why should I let anyone rain on my parade? I'm fine just the way I am!"

You may be fine as you are, but you can't see everything, and you don't know everything. Nobody does. The expression "to put in my two cents" exists for a reason. If several people drop two cents into your little tin cup, eventually it will add up. If everyone who cares about you offers solid words of advice, you'll have a broader, clearer picture of your dilemma, which will enable you to make better choices.

Notice I said everyone who cares about you. The reality is not all advice is heartfelt, and everyone doesn't wish you well. Sometimes it's hard to discern truly has your best interests at heart. At times your gut instinct is good enough, but often the only way to be certain is to observe the evolution of the friendship over time.

Have they been there when you needed them most? Would they feed your dog and water your plants if you went on vacation? Are they honest with you about themselves and about you? Do they flatter you instead of calling you out on your mistakes?

Think about a time when someone you cared about called you out over something you shouldn't have been doing. How did it feel? Were you angry or defensive, or were you open to their caring, loving criticism?

When friends or loved ones acknowledge your flaws, it doesn't mean they think they're perfect. Far from it. In fact, they have their own flaws. But for the sake of your relationship, don't make the mistake of responding to their criticism by lashing out with criticism of your own. That's not constructive, and it certainly won't help you improve. Now, if you have friends or loved ones who are always pointing out your flaws while never acknowledging their own; you may eventually want to have a conversation with them about that. But don't block the blessing that can likely

THE IMPORTANCE OF ME

be found in the constructive criticism they're throwing your way.

If it helps, wait awhile before you act. Negative feedback can sting, and you may not be in the proper mood to accept it, much less act on it. Our brains are designed to hear only the "criticism" part, causing us to miss the "constructive" part being offered as well.

If the criticism is designed to help rather than wound, as you think it through you may realize what the person was saying is right. Likewise, you may realize you are blessed to have people in your life who will attempt to plant positive seeds in you, something for which you should be grateful. When it's all said and done and the dust settles, you may even find yourself coming back and saying, "thank you" for the little nudge that turned you away from something negative and pointed you in a positive direction.

Okay. Now you may be wondering how to decide what advice to accept. Well, a good litmus test for me is to look at my friend and see how she's faring in life. Is she taking her own advice? How are things

43 | P a g e

going for her? You see, I won't take helpful hints about walking with my umbrella from someone who's always dashing in from the rain soaking wet! Or, to put it more bluntly, I have a friend who knows someone who once remarked, "I don't take dieting advice from fat folks." I know that's harsh. But the woman's husband was trying to chastise her about her diet when he himself is considerably overweight.

One of the areas in our lives in which it's most difficult for us to take advice is our intimate relationship. When you're deeply in love you want everyone else to love your man, too. That said, it cuts very badly to hear a friend or family member criticize him.

You know what I mean, don't you ladies? Your girlfriends will say they don't think he's right for you, but you aren't trying to hear that. They relay information about him from another source, such as he's got another girlfriend, his credit is bad or he's been accused of abuse, but as far as you're concerned they can't be talking about YOUR MAN. Of course, that's because your man is perfect – or as close to it as they come.

Honey, believe me. I've been there. Even though my man was abusive, I didn't entertain people talking to me about my husband. Now I could talk about him like a dog if I felt the need, but when it came to my girlfriends, I couldn't have heard them if they'd shouted in my ear at the top of their lungs.

When you're in denial about your man and don't want to listen to the truth, you might even fool yourself into thinking, *"Oh, they're just jealous because I have something wonderful and they don't."* We're all convinced the relationship we're in is the romance of the century, right? This is especially true when the relationship is brand new and squeaky clean.

But time has a way of revealing truths, and just as the honeymoon phase of a new romance wears off, eventually people begin to show you who they really are. And when your man starts showing his true colors, that's when you realize your friends weren't jealous but instead they were just looking out for you. What they said to you while you were blinded by love wasn't meant to hurt you; it was for your own good. That's when you understand the depth of love your friends have for you and that they're in your corner.

There's a saying, "Old people can see sitting down what you can't see standing up." It sounds funny but don't laugh! Younger generations like to think they invented love and sex and that nobody in the history of the universe has ever loved as hard as they do or has experienced what they're experiencing.

Come on. Now do you really believe that? When it comes to love and heartache, older folks, especially older women, have been there done that. Likewise, their observations, opinions and advice are filled with more knowledge than you can imagine. And the best part is they're willing to share it for free! So instead of muttering *"She's old and couldn't possibly understand what I'm going through,"* under your breath, try spending a few minutes listening to her. You just might be surprised at the wisdom she imparts.

Moreover, don't be fooled and say, "I'm a grownup. I'm not a kid, so why should I take advice from this old person?" You may be grown, but so am I. Still, there's nothing wrong with being smart enough to recognize when someone is offering you the benefit of their understanding – out of kindness and love.

And to younger women who are reading this, please understand that you really don't know everything. I mean no disrespect in saying that. I was once young, too, and thought I knew everything. However, I had to learn the hard way that I didn't. Please accept that I've lived longer than you and am in a better position to predict possible outcomes to certain situations. When I offer advice, I offer it with love, and I hope you receive it in that spirit.

Even so, after all is said and done remember you are in charge of *your* life. *You* are in control. When you're given advice, no matter how well-intentioned, if a voice deep in your heart whispers to that it's not right, you're certainly under no obligation to take the advice. I'm always open to listening to the opinions of someone I trust, but I also trust my instincts to know that if it's not for me, it's just not for me.

Sometimes when in doubt I pray about it, asking God to bless me with the insight to determine whether to stay my course or swerve in the direction of my friend's advice. In fact, I pray about everything.

My husband Terence is my best friend, and I can always count on him to point out things about me that I'm not seeing. He points them out directly, but in a kind manner. When he does this, I know he has my best interests at heart. I appreciate that and love him for it. I may not *like* him at every moment, as nobody gets along one hundred percent of the time. And that goes for even the best of marriages. But I absolutely do love him, and that's good enough for me.

Please understand this is real life, people, and not a Saturday morning cartoon. There will be times when your friends let you down. You'll go through trials with them and maybe even a period where you stop speaking to each other. Frankly, you may experience times when you think your friendship is over.

It's up to you to discern whether a particular friendship has run its course. And believe me. Some do. If you get to a point where you're deciding whether to continue a friendship, take some time to evaluate the importance of the relationship and what it means to your life. Think about what each of you has brought to the relationship. If you decide the friendship is important enough to continue it, no matter what caused the rift or the separation in the first place, mend fences with your friend. You could look at it as an economist would, as a simple matter of assets and liabilities: If your assets outweigh your liabilities, then it's a relationship worth saving. But if the scale tips in the other direction, well, honey, it's time to make some tough decisions and cut your losses. You often hear women lament about intimate relationships in which they stayed too long. Well, take it from one who knows. Sometimes, ladies, we stay in friendships with some of our girlfriends too long, too.

Ups and downs are a natural part of relationships. But forgiveness and healing are what friendship is about. When it comes to my friends, I constantly remind myself that though things between us aren't always pristine and hunky dory, I know they love me.

WHO ARE YOU?

I often ask myself, "Who are you?" And when I pose that question to myself, I come up with a variety of answers. I'm a mother. I'm a wife. I'm a sister. I'm a business owner. I'm a teacher. I'm a friend. And I'm even more than that. I'm many different things and wear many different hats. But what I do is only part of who I am.

Before you can go anywhere in your lives, you should decipher these three words: Who... Are... You? Decipher them, embrace your identity and understand it. In other words, outside of all the many hats we wear, who genuinely and authentically are we? What are all the elements that have come together to create us? You and me? What are the life experiences and challenges you've faced that have led you to this place? Who are the people sent by God to act upon your life to bring you here? These are questions I ponder routinely, and it's probably not a bad idea for you to ponder them as well.

Sometimes we have to sit and figure out what we're doing and why. In other words what is our purpose in life? But before we get there, we should pause to fully understand what "purpose" means. We hear the word bandied about a lot, and I'm pretty sure everyone who uses it has a different interpretation of it.

In my opinion, your purpose is your God-given talent that needs to be brought to fruition for you to live life to the fullest. In essence, it's the main thing that God intended for you to achieve while you're on this earth.

For many of us, our purpose comes naturally. We do it almost effortlessly. Your purpose brings out the best in you and helps you be the truest version of yourself. Your purpose also brings you happiness and great and abiding contentment.

Sadly, a lot of us aren't sure of our purpose, in part because we're still trying to figure ourselves out. Some of us may know deep down what our purpose is; however, we try to ignore it or act as though we don't know because it might not be as "sexy" or as pleasurable as some other things we like to do instead.

Other things may give us more pleasure than our purpose, but that pleasure is just temporary and can turn into an ever-increasing chasm between our present selves and the people we're meant to be. Sometimes we need to give up our bad habits and addictions to ensure we clear a path to becoming the person *God* wants us to be – rather than remaining the person *we* want to be.

Your path to self-discovery is individual to you, and no one else can come up with a recipe for finding *your* purpose. When I'm counseling people, I always ask them this question: "If all your material needs were met and all your financial problems were erased, what would you do with your life?" The one thing you would keep on doing is probably closely connected to your purpose, so I suggest you begin with this simple question and take it from there.

I hope you understand your answer will be different depending on where you are in life. If someone had asked me that question a few years ago, I know unequivocally I would have said I was going shopping or traveling – or both!

Today, thank God, I'm in a place where I can answer this question without being so materialistic. You may be wondering how you get to that point. The answer is through prayer and meditation, which brings clarity and takes your focus away from material things. Even if you aren't a praying person, meditation and contemplation are there for you to participate in and grow from.

WHAT DO I MEAN WHEN I SAY GOD"?

Although I'm a Christian, I don't think it's fair to restrict myself to the Christian definition of God, because I believe we're all entitled to our own beliefs and perceptions, as well as our own relationships with Him.

I say "He" when I talk about God, but I understand there are women whose concept of God is feminine, or even genderless. I also know there are people who don't necessarily believe in a personal God, but who recognize and accept the notion of a higher power.

So, whenever I say "God," please feel free to understand this or interpret it however you see fit. I'm not here to judge you or compete with you. I've written this book in the spirit of love, in hopes of empowering you.

PROTECTION

We all have an inherent sense of something out there bigger than ourselves. This "something" guides us, even whispers to us when we're doing wrong. And that "still small voice" is one we all must listen to for our own protection and the protection of others.

You may not agree with me, but I believe whether or not we pray there's a force out there that protects us. In my professional life, I meet people who went through hard times without praying. Yet, after they emerge from their difficulty and look back, they admit there was someone or something looking out for them and protecting them. They also acknowledge what they went through could have been much worse.

Does this mean people who experience devastating loss and tragedy aren't under God's protection? Do bad things happen when you don't pray? Of course not. We all encounter loss and tragedy at some point in our lives – some more than others.

Instead of blaming ourselves, we must remember there are things beyond our power. Just as we can't influence the rising or setting of the sun, we can't prevent some painful events from occurring in our lives. Life happens. Most of the time, it's good. However, sometimes there's sadness.

PURPOSE AND DESTINY

What's the connection between purpose and destiny?

Your purpose is your God-given talent. Your destiny is what's meant to happen to you – what's preordained. Your destiny is God's long-term plan, a map He's already drawn for your entire life. This is why I don't believe you can – or should – change your destiny in any major way. Attempting to do so is equivalent to wrenching the reins of your life out of God's hands. That sense of control may sound exciting, but none of us can see into the future. When we think we're in control – though we never, truly are – we are most likely, in all actuality, be steering ourselves away from something wonderful. Having a cocky, bull-headed attitude can mess up your destiny.

Negatively altering our destiny would be tragic, because the alternative path we choose isn't God-driven. When God doesn't have a hand in guiding our lives, that leaves us further and further from where He wants us to be.

THE IMPORTANCE OF ME

I believe we know who we are meant to be on an instinctive level, because that intention has been implanted in us since birth. But it takes maturity to recognize and understand this intention, and for many of us, attaining that maturity takes a long time.

As we grow our self-awareness grows, and this intention is brought to fruition through the things we do, the decisions we make. Once our self-awareness increases, we begin to fully understand and identify what God intended for us.

God's intentions for our lives are why I firmly believe nobody is born into this world with a criminal mentality. Evil is learned.

Children born into dire circumstances may be exposed to huge negative influences, and they need adults to guide them and help them rise beyond their tough circumstances. The best way adults can help children born into rough situations is by offering them positive alternatives. Take my life as an example. I was exposed to teen sex, teen pregnancy, poverty and domestic violence. Yet with some effort – and a whole

63 | P a g e

lot of self-awareness and determination AND adults stepping in to show me the way from time to time – I was able to extricate myself from that entanglement.

But I was fortunate. Children cannot rise from their circumstances on their own. It's up to us as adults to reach out to these children and help them. We adults need to put things in place so they can be helped, especially in the schools. The earlier we can identify children in need, the sooner we can save them – particularly those of us who are mental health care practitioners. As a society, it's our job to protect the children.

APPEARANCE

We live in a vain, shallow world. We spend far too much time trying to force ourselves to fit into the narrow definition of "beautiful" that's been set out for us. Listen, ladies, let me be the first to tell you it's frustrating and it's fruitless. I'm not saying we women shouldn't dress well or have our nails done every once in a while. And I'm certainly not knocking lipstick. Those little things we do to make us feel better about ourselves are fine, and how we do them is a matter of our choice. If you want to straighten your hair, go for it honey! If you don't want to straighten your hair, rock that natural look! Just remember none of this defines you. Instead, who you are and how you go about achieving your purpose defines you.

Make sure the decisions you make are your own versus ones influenced by the constant barrage of negative brain-washing that overwhelms us every time we turn on our TVs or log onto the Internet. Even our friends and family are sometimes guilty of trying to bend us to their idea of how we should look on the outside.

Everyone loves to tell us what we should look like, how we should dress, what our skin tone should be, how we should wear our hair and even how big our butts should be.

This obsession devalues us. All of us, even "perfect" celebrities, have flaws. Some people go out of their way, even enduring great pain and expense, to change things about ourselves. Yes, I'm talking about plastic surgery.

But why? Isn't our appearance part of our destiny? Don't we look the way God wants us to look? This obsession with our looks shifts our attention from what we should really be focusing on. So why don't we simply appreciate ourselves? If your butt is flat, appreciate it. Don't like your lips or your eyes or your hair? Honey, appreciate them, too. You look exactly the way God wants you to look.

Now smile. See? That's God's own natural beauty remedy!

PROCRASTINATION

Ultimately, our goal is to live a life of authenticity. A life that brings joy, happiness and peace. Unfortunately, it doesn't happen because we're too busy trying to figure what we're going to do next.

We often second-guess ourselves. At some point, all of us have come to a place where we're so unsure about what to do next that we do nothing at all. Our tires are stuck in the mud and we can go neither forward nor backward. We don't know where to go, how to go, or who to go with.

So, we do nothing.

How do we get unstuck? How do we go forward?

We begin by acknowledging a lot of this paralysis is caused by fear of failure, fear of embarrassment or fear of being angry with ourselves if we fail. If this happens, remind yourself the only way to move forward is through trial and error. Mistakes will happen, but each one represents an opportunity to learn. Each one takes you closer to your goal.

When your car gets stuck in the mud, don't you call AAA? Well, when you get stuck isn't there someone upon whom you can call? Absolutely! You can call on your significant other, your family, your friends or last but certainly not least God.

INSTINCTIVELY DOING THE RIGHT THING

Have you ever done something you knew you shouldn't? Was it easy? Did you just go out and do it? Or did it require planning? How much effort did you put into working out how you were going to do it, how not to get caught, what kinds of excuses, or even lies, you'd have to make up to get out of trouble if you got caught? Whose feelings might get hurt? What penalties would you have to pay, and how do you avoid paying them?

Are you tired yet? How does that wrong activity compare, in terms of expending energy, with what would have happened if you'd done the right thing? Not too well, huh?

It takes much less effort to do the right thing, simply because the knowledge and effort it takes already resides within us. Knowing what's right is instinctive, because it's part of God's plan for who we're supposed to be.

PLEASING PEOPLE

Many of us get so caught up in pleasing people. We aim to please our bosses, our church members, our friends, our families and so many different people while we're not even pleasing ourselves.

Yet we most definitely should!

You may think pleasing yourself is selfish, but nothing could be farther from the truth. If you don't take care of yourself, how are you going to be equipped to take care of others? Have you ever flown? When the flight attendants are giving instructions and explaining what to do should the oxygen masks become necessary, they always say if you're traveling with a small child or person needing assistance, put your mask on first before trying to help that person. Self-care and self-love should always be high on our agendas. Even though it's hard to do, we sometimes have to set our burdens aside for a minute to give ourselves time to refresh and regroup.

One of the ways I take care of myself is by ensuring I eat properly. Also, I get a massage and my nails done weekly. It may seem like such a little thing, but you know how much being pampered can lift your mood, right? When things get too overwhelming, I say to my husband, "Hey, it's time for a vacation. Let's go!" Your mind will tell you when it's time to do something for *you*. I also read my Bible regularly to feed my spirit, because I simply can't neglect that.

And if there are people talking behind your back questioning why you're going for a facial when you have so much work to do, just ignore them. How and when you take care of you is not for them to decide. You know what you need to get yourself back on track, and you're entitled to a little guilt-free me-time occasionally. Take yourself out to dinner, girl! Take a day off of work and go see a movie in the middle of the day, when there might be 10 people in the entire theatre. Doing things, *you* like to do are what you must do for self-care.

But ladies, please don't forget about couples time. You and your significant other need to constantly re-commit to spending time together and to focusing on your relationship. Sometimes my husband and I are so busy that there's potential for neglect in our relationship. Fortunately, that's when we stop and say, "Hey! We need to focus on our marriage! We need to focus on our home!" That's part of self-care, too.

We also have to remember that we're expected to please God. It's a vital element for our growth and advancement. When we get to the point where we're so focused on other things that we forget about pleasing God, we can hit a brick wall head on.

I know because I've been there several times. We all have. But I don't let it discourage me. I may not be one hundred percent where God wants me to be, but I'm trying to get there and believe I will.

THAT AH-HA MOMENT

You may have a problem, an issue or a pending decision that's been weighing heavily on your mind. You turn it over and turn it over in your head and then, all of a sudden, you experience an aha moment. You see a solution! You visualize a path way forward!

That "aha moment" as I like to call it comes from God. It makes us stop and think about what we're doing and why we're doing it. It also makes us wonder what's the purpose of what we're doing. We start revamping our thoughts and doing things differently. But changing the way we do things we've done all our life, things we've grown accustomed to or do the way we do because that's what we thought we were supposed to do, can be tricky.

Often, our idea of what we're "supposed to do" comes from sources outside ourselves including the media, the church, our families, our spouses and our upbringing. It's hard to know if we're being manipulated, and even harder to find the strength to go against these deeply ingrained thoughts.

How do we identify what needs to change? Try to identify things you've been doing repeatedly that have brought you nothing but grief, pain and destruction. Think about walls against which you keep banging your head. Those are pretty good red flags right there, flags that make you say to yourself, "Wow, this isn't working. I need to do something different!"

Breaking old thought patterns and habits can be hard, but it helps to be surrounded by positive people. Immerse yourself in positive things you like to do, which may involve taking a step back to examine what you're doing, who you're doing it with and why you're doing it.

When you do this, your thought processes change and you can steer clear of the bad road you were heading down and get onto a better path. Sometimes God even gives you a little nudge. You may have been stagnating in a safe, comfy place for too long, knowing there's more out there for you yet lacking the motivation or drive to step forward. You might have known you were in a dead-end, but God will take away that cushy spot and make you uncomfortable enough to move. It may not feel like it at the time, but it will all be for your betterment.

It can even be scary knowing change is coming, but it's time to stop being complacent and step up. Your aha moment may bring the opportunity to do something you've been yearning to do for a long time but just couldn't accomplish.

Indeed, an aha moment can be a game changer!

You can nudge your "it" along without just sitting passively and waiting. I get there through prayer and contemplation, thinking things over in the quiet of my mind. Notice I said *thinking* things over versus worrying about them. Worrying gets you nowhere. I always try to sit quietly for fifteen minutes every day and just be still, calming my mind and listening for God's voice. And very often, He speaks.

WHAT IS YOUR GIFT?

Sometimes aha moments verify that God has placed a gift in you, one you're meant to bring forth for others to see. Usually the gift has been inside you since conception. Sometimes it's easy to identify because it's a skill or a passion that comes easy to you. Whatever your gift, you just know it's something you're meant to do.

My gift is helping others. From my earliest childhood days, I knew I was a helper, destined to assist others along their paths. I still believe I'm supposed to lead by example, and that's how I try to live my life. In fact, a desire to help others is a large part of the reason I wrote this book.

Sometimes we realize our gifts late in life. It happens when God opens your eyes to the existence of something you may not have been aware of. When that happens... hooray! Praise God! Seize it and run with it, woman!

Your gifts are given to you so you can do what's necessary to bring peace and joy not only to yourself but first and foremost to God. And make no mistake about it. God should be first in your life. If He's not happy with what you're doing, you can't be happy, either. In the same vein, if your higher power is telling you to do something and you don't, there will be consequences. One of those consequences is that you won't find peace.

Once you discover your gifts and begin to manifest them, others will be able to genuinely see who you are as a person. But you have to want this. You have to search for and seek this. And you have to find it. Sometimes you will have to go through so many layers to get to that particular place, but you can do it, because you know God is with you.

It's not going to happen overnight. Sometimes it takes years of effort, dedication and trial and error for things to work out. And lots of people think the "error" in "trial and error" is a bad thing, but it's not. Errors are wonderful. Errors are your friend. Because errors are the only way to learn what doesn't work for you. They're like a huge sign hanging before you that says, "Stop! Turn around. Go another way."

And so you try again. As long as you take what you've learned from your mistake and apply it to what you're doing, you'll eventually have a positive outcome.

BACKSLIDING

Once you get to the place you want to be, there's always the danger of backsliding, of losing your traction or the energy that propelled you forward. Don't let that happen! Remind yourself about where you've come from and where you still intend to go. Think about the bad habits and activities you've so proudly left behind and tell yourself sternly that you're no longer that same person who did those things. This is where supportive, like-minded people can help, too.

It's important to stop giving ourselves excuses to backslide. Everything that crops up shouldn't demand your full attention. If you let it, you'll wind up spinning like a top.

It's up to you to prioritize and to save your energy for what matters and what will best serve you on your road to self-discovery.

BAD HABITS AND ADDICTIONS

Sometimes we find ourselves being held back by forces that seem intent on keeping us from reaching our personal promised land. We return again and again to habits we know are bad, habits like procrastination, wasting time and self-doubt. More tangible habits like eating badly or alcohol abuse can entangle us and distract us from our goals.

We need to constantly be vigilant while devising strategies that work for us to shake those habits or, at least, to keep them at bay.

One thing I'd like to point out is there's a difference between a bad habit and an addiction. Addictions don't refer only to drugs or alcohol but instead include a huge range of substances or situations that are difficult to shake once they get you in their grip. With addictions, you wind up hurting yourself and others as well. (For example, if you're addicted to gambling and you constantly spend your mortgage and car payment money in the casino, sooner or later unless you have a hefty nest egg in the bank, your house will be foreclosed and your car will be repossessed.)

If this is the case with you, meaning you have a harmful addiction, you need help. You may think you can beat your addiction alone, but you can't. Seek mental health counseling and spiritual support. The problem might look too great for you to surmount, but with help you can. With the proper help, no problem or addiction is insurmountable.

And if you haven't started using them, please stay away from addictive substances. We live in an experiential society, where we feel we have to try everything. But the advice and experiences of those who've gone through addiction and come out on the other side is worth more than gold. Please, whatever you do, heed their warnings.

LIVING A LIFE THAT IS NOT SO TRUE

It's not easy realizing we've lived a "false" life. By that, I mean a life built on appearances, one in which you care more about what other people think of you than about what truly matters.

Believe me; I did a lot of that during my first marriage. I put on a persona like other people put on winter coats. It covered everything. It hid the truth. Because I was so desperate for people to think my life was great, I was willing to blind them and me to what was going on. Honestly, it would have killed me for other people to know I was in an abusive relationship.

Even in less serious situations, this false façade is tempting. We have come to the point where we allow social media and other shallow forms of positive reinforcement to nurture our very souls. We let the media, society and even the church tell us how we're supposed to be. We let other people fill our heads with their idea of who and what we should be.

Come on! You're better than that! To make a difference, you must be truly aware of who you are as an individual and work diligently to bring the best version of that person forward – in spite of what people think. Mindless conformity may be the prevailing culture, but you need to declare out loud that's not the culture for you.

PURPOSE

The moment you find out your purpose is the moment you really start living. When you trust and believe in God, everything falls into place.

This doesn't mean you're going to be consistently happy, or that everything in your life will be perfect. Sometimes things will be rough. There will be moments of pain, sadness, fear and grief. After all, we're human. And tough times don't always mean you've done something wrong. Sometimes, things just happen.

But happiness comes from within. A lot of our happiness is based not so much on our external circumstances but rather on how we react to those circumstances.

You have to get to that point, but everybody doesn't get to it right away. Some reach that point early while others reach it later in life. Whenever you get to that point, it's the right time. The key is patience! Oftentimes we get so caught up in thinking we're supposed to be at certain places at certain times in our lives. Not necessarily. You're right where you need to be at the time you're there. We must endure several stages of each issue we face before learning why we're doing what we're doing – and for what purpose.

But at the same time, this isn't a passive process. It's not going to leap out at you when you turn a corner. You need to be an active participant in your search for self-betterment, and you need to keep at it. You need to surround yourself with your passion. Does anything good come from procrastination? No!

Everything, from birth right up to that aha moment, was put in place by your higher power. He gives you the seeds, but you're the one who has to go out and plant them.

When you get there, you have the luxury of reflecting and seeing how far you came. That is your story, your revelation, your awakening. When you go back and review your life and see the positive and the negative, you allow the positive to reinforce you while drawing examples from the negative to remind you why you'll never go back there again. Then you can exclaim I SURVIVED AND NOW I'M LIVING, TRULY LIVING IN MY PURPOSE!

You dream while you sleep, don't you? Well, I'm sure you dream while you're awake, too. And if you have the same dream over and over, that's your higher power telling you it's something you need to look into.

You have birthed your dream because it came to you while you were taking each step set out for you. The path you took was meticulously prepared for you, and events in your life were designed to mold you into the person you are today. The universe always put things in place for a reason.

But how do you recognize these steps are the ones you're supposed to follow? It's hard, but you need to let your intuition guide you. It helps if your relationship with your higher power is close enough to allow you to know and trust the signs. This is especially important when you come to a crossroads. Which path would God want you to take?

I suggest you pray about it. Praying always helps me whenever I'm confused or I misunderstand something, because God is never the author of confusion.

The idea of a prepared path sounds like predestination, but that doesn't mean you don't have a choice. You aren't forced to make a choice or do anything you don't want to. But it's at the moment of choosing the right path, the one your higher power intended, that you step into your destiny. In other words, God won't force you. You have to see the road, tap into your inner self to know which is right and which is wrong and decide to step onto it.

Sometimes stepping into the unknown can be scary. Nobody knows what's at the end of the path, which can be tough. Other people might look at you and say, "Look at her, jumping through all those hoops," but you know it's worth it. You might even find that your excitement and adrenaline are going to push you along anyway!

THE IMPORTANCE OF ME

Just do me and yourself a favor and don't let your fears stop you. If you do, you're in essence telling God you don't trust him. Likewise, you're just setting yourself up for the consequences of inaction or robbing yourself of the positivity and success that can come into being if only you had the courage to do what you need to do. If you aren't happy with the choices you're making, you're basically scared to live your life. You're sabotaging yourself and stunting your own growth.

When you finally arrive at that point, you might even want to pinch yourself and ask *is this really happening.* Yes, it's happening! Now live. Go and *do.* Spread whatever gift you have. Step out of your comfort zone and let others see it.

You can do the impossible. You can do the unthinkable. Walk through that door. Don't be scared. Turn the knob, open the door and walk through it. BLISS is waiting for you on the other side!

Living life to the fullest is the best feeling ever. The negative things and negative people no longer

102 | P a g e

matter at this point. When you're in this state, you don't get caught up on stupid, pointless or petty things. You're in a different mind-set. Letting those old thoughts bog you down is just a waste of time.

You enjoy what you do. Even others can see you're a new person. Of course, there will be some people who come and say, "I remember when…"

The question is are they remembering your past to celebrate with you how far you've come, or are they trying to drag you back there, back down into the mud with them? If they want to celebrate with you, enjoy! If they're trying to hurt you by throwing your past in your face, remind them that it's just that – your past. Remind them and keep it moving.

Yes, your past has shaped you into the person you are today, but you don't have to live it anymore. And those people that reference who you were back then simply haven't found who they are yet. They can't embrace who you are, and that's where you pull off those layers. If it sounds hard, don't worry because God will remove the layers for you.

It can be painful to admit, but sometimes those "layers" standing between you and success might actually be people in your life who, out of jealousy, possessiveness or simple cruelty will bog you down and impede your progress.

Your body will tell you if you're in the wrong crowd, because you'll be overcome with discomfort. You just need to listen and be more aware so you'll do the right thing when the time comes.

It might be difficult to shake these people, especially if you've known them for a long time. But I've often found that God either gives you the strength to break those ties or arranges for those relationships to come to a natural and conclusive end. It might be hard, but you need to remember these people can't go where you're going.

I'm not advocating you hurt anyone. I hate hurting people. Sometimes I ask God to simply make it so they can be peaceably removed from my life, without issues or hard feelings. This way when we come together in the future, it won't be awkward, painful or uncomfortable.

And if that doesn't happen, meaning actively ending the relationship or giving the person a much lesser role in your life falls upon your shoulders, be kind. Be gentle. Remember, it's not what you say oftentimes but instead it's how you say it. Most of all be honest. Lying to someone is disrespectful, and I'm sure they'd prefer the truth just as would you.

But understand you won't be lost or alone. Oh no! God also fills voids in our lives by introducing us to different caliber of people who share our goals and values, people who are willing to help us along and also willing to accept help when they need it. You need to spend time around people who think like you and are doing things and making strides just like you. Your tribe determines your vibe.

It doesn't mean you will all get there at the same pace. It happens at different times for everyone.

Don't be like Lot's wife and look back at the people you're leaving behind. Not everyone is meant to go with you on your journey. People you were at one time close with might not be on that journey with you. Some people have to be removed from your life for you to continue living your purpose. In other words, to continue being yourself may require letting go of some dead weight.

Now, of course you'll be called everything but a child of God, but it's okay. Remind yourself that as long as you know your purpose, who you're serving and why you're doing what you're doing, it doesn't matter. They, too, will understand once they realize their own purpose, once they have their own aha moment. But until then, keep striving and doing what you must for yourself and those who will be recipients of your purpose and gift.

Live in that moment. Embrace it.

When someone comes to you and asks whether you think you're better than he or she is or whether you think you're brand new, your answer can be really simple. "No, I don't think I'm brand new. But I'm better than I was because I'm not the person I used to be."

You're not being arrogant so don't worry about coming across as such. Eventually, you'll be able to point others in the right direction. You can tell them, "When your time comes, you'll understand." And you can continue walking into your destiny. You're doing something you thought you'd never do. It's okay. You are you.

FRIENDSHIP

Most women will say friendship is an important part of their life. For me, friendship is the state of being a friend. Sounds simplistic? Not really. The definition depends on who you ask. Some say friendship is unconditional love, accepting a person for who she is, regardless of what she has going on in her life. People have different views on what friendship and what it entails.

No matter your view of friendship, I think most would agree the word itself comes with a lot of expectations. Can you trust the person you call friend? Will she be there in your time of need? Those are difficult questions to answer, but a good indication of how someone will treat you in the future is how she has responded to you in the past.

A relationship considered sacred by both parties will most likely withstand any storm. We all desire this type of friendship, and many are lucky enough to have it. Even so, there are some that don't understand what it means to be a friend. So, let's talk it out!

Understanding the bond of friendship and all that comes with it takes dedication and practice. It's not something that happens overnight. It may take weeks, months or sometimes even years. But whatever the time frame, it is a bond that's pretty tough to break and the time invested will certainly be worth it.

Once you develop a close, sacred bond of friendship with another person, it doesn't mean the two of you won't disagree, argue or even fall out from time to time. But even if disagreements, arguments or fallings out occur, if the friendship is true you'll find yourself together again in due time, in the spirit of forgiveness, cementing your bond.

Friends add a lot to our lives. They make us laugh. They cry with us when we're sad. They lend listening ears when we just need to vent or get something off of our chests. And when we feel the need to release some stress by acting crazy, they're right there beside us acting crazy, too. Friends remember the silly things we did as a child and sometimes don't hesitate to bring up those things at

THE IMPORTANCE OF ME

the most inopportune times. Yes, that's right. Friends sometimes embarrass us. But most of all, friends love us and care for us. True friends are like family – only you're not related to them by blood. The real beauty of friends is, unlike your family, your get to choose them. You make a conscious decision to have friends in your life, to invite them in your "inner circle" and to share with them. I don't know about you, but the way I see it, there's nothing like a good, true friend.

My friends have listened to me rant and rave about all of the issues I've had in my life, including those that still linger. It goes without saying friendship is a special bond between people who share some similarities as well as differences. You don't have to like the same things or believe in the same ideologies to be friends. If everyone you loved was just like you, how boring would that be?

Coming from dissimilar backgrounds can actually be an advantage, as each person brings her experiences, beliefs and perspectives to the friendship. In friendships people share their experiences to help

112 | P a g e

THE IMPORTANCE OF ME

each other. These characteristics mold the friendship and make it rewarding to both parties.

Yet, it's not uncommon to reach a point in our lives when we question whether we have true friends or whether we're alone. At times you may find yourself wondering, is *anyone there for me? What would happen to me in a time of crisis?*

God answers this question every time, by putting the right people in your life to help you through the rough patches. He shows you who's there in our time of need. God makes it plain because when you're down and out, your true friends surface. It's funny, because during the hard times true friends just show up, even if you've gone months or years without speaking.

You might be wondering why you should remain friends with someone who hasn't made the effort to see you in a long time. Well, you know how life is. Sometimes we just get too overwhelmed to reach out, but true friends are always there in our hearts and are just a phone call away when our busy

113 | P a g e

lives give us a break and we can take a few moments to give them a call.

You don't have to be on the phone day in and day out with your friends. True friendship is one where you can pick up right where you left off from the last conversation, whether that conversation happened a month ago or years ago. True, genuine friendship stands the test of time.

God sends special people in our lives at different times. Some of us are fortunate enough to develop enduring friendships that begin when we're children, but that doesn't discount the relationships we build later in life. At different stages of our lives friends come and go. Indeed, friends come in our lives at different seasons of our lives.

As a young child, I didn't understand the meaning of friendship. In fact, it was foreign to me. Sure, I played with other kids all of the time, but because of my life circumstances I didn't understand what friendship meant – not until I became an adult.

For me, friendship means being there for someone during the good days and bad days.

There was one particular friend that was there for me during my difficult childhood, and today she and I share the longest friendship out of our circle. We grew up in the same housing project. Even during the dark days of my first pregnancy, she was supportive. She never shunned me or spoke ill of me behind my back like others did. Her constant message was, "Let me help you get through this ordeal."

During my marriage, my ex-husband tried to keep us separated. He tried mightily to scare her away so I would be isolated and more vulnerable to him. Even after our divorce, the resentment he felt for her was still there.

After moving into my new place, I had a cookout. My ex-husband showed up and the fact that he resented her presence was obvious. He gave her a menacing look that conveyed, "What're you doing here? You need to leave!" But she stood up to him and shot him a look that said: "I'm not going anywhere! I got my girl's back!"

She and I see each other often, share meals at each other's houses and talk by phone every weekend. She doesn't get caught up in my past or present. She just is. She's been a part of everything I do and I love her for it.

I remember one time at a family gathering to celebrate her mom's birthday; we started reminiscing about my early experiences. My second husband, Terence, was shocked. I'd told him about my past, but until that day he had no idea it'd been that bad! The sharing of things I'd gone through brought it home to him and made things crystal clear as they say. Hearing all of that came as a shock to Terence, who'd grown up in a happy, stable and loving family. He couldn't conceive of a child living through anything else. To him, parents love their children and children are treated well by their parents – plain and simple. Period.

It's funny, but sometimes I'll receive a text message from her reminding me that our friendship is the longest among all of our relationships. The words mean so much to me, every time they pop up on my phone.

We don't talk every day, and we don't see each other frequently as we have our own lives. But when we do get together, our conversation picks up where we left off and continues to build until the next time we meet. Every time we're together it's like a breath of fresh air. It's freeing and life-affirming knowing our bond is there and isn't going anywhere. She is special to me and always will be. She taught me so much about being my truest self and not getting caught up in worldly things. She helped me understand how not to let my past define my future. I'm forever grateful to her, and every opportunity I get to reciprocate the love she's shown me, I'm more than happy to take it.

Some friendships develop as we grow into adulthood, or even later on in life. Even though friendships that happen later don't have the rich history of our childhoods, they still mean so much to us. Sometimes, adult friendships hold a special significance because when we're older we understand each other's trials with more clarity and compassion. It's really good to have someone who understands the things we're going through because they're either going through them, too, or have already gone through them.

PERSEVERANCE

Many times, we're halted by the need to make a decision about a challenge, an encounter, a painful or unpleasant situation or something unforeseen. How we embrace these challenges can make or break us; it all depends on our approach to the problem.

Have you ever noticed you can't spell the word perseverance without the word severe? Severe is defined in Merriam-Webster's dictionary as "rigorous in restraint; strongly critical or condemnatory; inflicting physical discomfort."

How is this relevant? Well, please hear me out. Throughout our history and even today, our people have endured *severe* circumstances and *persevered* to reach the destination God has ordained for us. From soldiers at war, to slaves fighting for their freedom to single parents, we have persevered. Whether you've struggled to get by and make ends meet because of job cuts or financial losses, everyone at one time or another has been forced to persevere. And the only way to do this is to be equipped with the necessary tools to endure these "severe" circumstances.

Allow me to pause for a minute and reference a text that fits perfectly in this chapter: James 1:12 NIV. The scripture says, "Blessed is the one who perseveres under trial because, having stood the test, that person will receive the crown of life that the Lord has promised to those who love him."

Sometimes we feel as though tests and trials shouldn't happen to us. But why not? What makes us so special that we should be exempt from the trials of life? Why do we think we're so much better than our neighbor that we should be given a pass on tests and trials, enabling us to continue living happy lives while they go through?

I'm sorry. But if that's what you're waiting for, let me be the first to tell you it's not going to happen. Job endured many trials and was a righteous man who God loved, so we, too, should be able to persevere through our trials and come out as conquerors.

What about you? How much are you willing to take? Can you or will you endure the test that is or will be placed before you?

THE GRIEF CYCLE

The Grief Cycle, as outlined by Elisabeth Kubler-Ross, explains the process that many individuals experience when grieving. This grief is not associated only with death or dying but can also be applied to the end of relationships, financial hardships, job losses, disability or sickness.

Let's take a better look at it here.

Denial: Conscious or unconscious refusal to accept facts or information related to the situation

Anger: A negative, intense emotional response to self or others, especially friends/family

Bargaining: Negotiating with God or other higher or religious being or person (depending on the situation) in an attempt to resolve the problem

Depression: Includes feelings of sadness, loneliness, regret, fear, etc.

Acceptance: An understanding and/or grasp of the situation.

Remember that although the stages usually follow each other in the order listed above, the reality is they can affect us in any order. There's also no limit to how long each stage lasts. For some it may be hours or days, while for others it may take weeks or months. Don't let that bother you as you're not bound to anyone's schedule. Your grief is personal to you. How you work through it is entirely up to you.

But remember to lean on your support network! Family, friends, counselors and God are all there for you.

CHOICE

We make choices daily, whether they're right or wrong. We choose to get up early or sleep in late; to attend an event we aren't keen on; to take a new job, to move to a new house or to take a course.

Sometimes it's not whether a choice you make is "good" but whether it's good *for you*, and good for you *at that moment*. Choices may be made at the spur of the moment, but please know they always have consequences.

I'll give you an example of a choice I made that had life-changing repercussions for me. I was invited to a motivational seminar and, to be honest, I wasn't crazy about the idea. Nonetheless, I accepted the invitation anyway. That small choice to push past my own unwillingness was followed by another choice – to go onstage and speak. Getting on that stage turned out to be my first step along a journey that led to me becoming a motivational speaker.

See? One step led to another. One choice led to another. If I'd refused to go to the seminar, giving in to whatever was holding me back, I would never have had the opportunity to make all of the subsequent choices that helped bring me to where I am today.

We're also faced with the choice to persevere during difficult times or just throw in the towel. What we choose at these junctures in our lives can have echoes for years to come, so we must choose carefully and wisely.

Of course, there will be times when giving up seems so much easier. Times when saying, "I simply don't understand algebra and never will. I might as well just drop the class" is so much easier than hanging in there, studying harder and finding a tutor. Persevering through the tough times can be daunting but realizing your inner strength can provide you with that extra *oomph* you need to continue moving forward.

"To be, or not to be: that is the question." Even Hamlet expressed the pain of life, and the difficulty he had deciding whether to go on or give up. He talks about floundering in a "sea of troubles" … the reality of living. Here again lies the choice we have – to paddle through the sea of troubles we encounter or allow the sharks to attack, overthrow and dismember our objectives. Maybe the question should be to persevere or not to persevere?

Since your life is different from mine your obstacles are different from mine, although we may share some commonalities. But it's the sheer diversity of humanity that makes it so hard to predict what obstacles may come, and how we may need to persevere through them.

For instance, two acquaintances of mine, Nancy and Sue, were given only a two-week notice that the plant where they work will be closing. Understandably, they're in disbelief. Both ladies have a mortgage, the usual bills and a family to help provide for. Immediately after learning the devastating news, Nancy begins revamping her resume and starts sending out feelers for a new job. Sue, on the other hand, allows the two weeks to pass without taking proactive steps. Before she realizes it, the weeks have turned into months, and she still hasn't begun searching for a job. She hasn't accepted the reality that she's no longer employed and is stuck between the denial and anger stages of the stages of grief.

We understand that each person handles situations differently. We also understand that, many times, emotional distress may hang us up, leaving us unable to act or even think. How we react to stress can affect how quickly or slowly we proceed or persevere though situations. I'm not saying we don't need a mental break, a healing or a thoughtful pause to ease us through the process, but we also shouldn't allow that break to become a permanent disengagement.

As for that mental break, there are so many options open to you that you have no excuse not to take one. It doesn't have to be complicated. It can be as simple as a short (or long!) walk, or a few deep breathing exercises. For a longer hiatus, maybe you could consider a visit to a spa, or even a brief holiday? Whatever it is, however you do it, take the time you need for yourself.

But don't take too long. When the time is right to get back out there, get back out there!

We have to trust the process. What does that mean? Regardless of how quickly or slowly we handle the situation, we need to handle it. And in some cases, speed matters, too. We can't afford to let chances fly past us because we're too slow to react.

Outcomes, successes and testimonies don't happen overnight; they are part of a process. Hence, in defining "perseverance," Merriam-Webster stresses that it takes, *"continued* effort to do or achieve something, despite difficulties, failure or opposition". With this in mind, do you think Sue has persevered though the circumstance surrounding her job loss?

To be, or not to be. To persevere or not. It's up to you. It's your life, your choice and your decision. Can you handle it? Or will you remain dormant, unmovable? It's not how fast you make it through that matters most. What matters most is that you make it through in spite of whatever stands in your way.

FAITH

"Now, faith is the substance of things hoped for, the evidence of things not seen." Hebrews 11:1

Faith has always been a major, driving influence in my life. It kept me uplifted through the tough times and justified my joy during the good times. Therefore, please allow me to share my thoughts on it with you.

Even as a young girl, I knew something more, something wonderful was available to me if only I asked for it. Before I was able to put it into words, I understood there was something – or someone – protecting us and looking out for us and that it was interested in me and cared about me.

There was one event in my early life in which those vague, trusting feelings inside me finally solidified and I understood what it really meant to have faith.

It was on my seventh birthday. Because of the circumstances of my early life, I never had a reason to expect much, not even on my birthday. I can't remember ever having a birthday celebration at that age: no party, no presents and certainly no cake.

On that particular birthday, however, I wanted a cake. And I didn't want just any cake. You see, there had been a drawing for a birthday cake through the local radio station, *WSTP*, and someone in my family had entered my name. I wanted to win that cake!

And girlfriend, I can't tell you how much I wanted it. All day I dreamed about it. I prayed and prayed, and I understood that my prayers were floating upward to a higher power.

I wanted that cake so badly I could taste it. To my mind, that cake was more than just a heap of sugar roses. It meant love and appreciation. Having that cake would mean someone loved me and valued me. Having that cake would mean I was special.

Waiting was hard, but I knew I would win the cake. I knew it. I knew it. I knew it. When I heard my name called on the radio station, my faith was confirmed. There *was* someone who loved me, someone who wanted me to have only good things. And I knew that person was God. No one else could have done that.

My mom collected it and brought it home. It was pink and green – my favorite colors – and I felt like it had been made just for me. I probably still have a photo of me holding it. We didn't have a party, but it sure tasted good!

Looking back, the day I heard my name announced as the winner of the cake was the day my faith began. Having faith at such a young age was a blessing. It was a source of strength and encouragement and a refuge through everything I faced.

I always knew something much stronger than me was in place. I couldn't explain it, but something was there.

Looking back over my life, I realize trials and tribulations come only to make us strong – just like the agony of waiting on that cake! Despite the struggles I endured during my marriage, thoughts of doing bigger and better things were always at the forefront of my mind. My goal was always a better life for myself and my children, and that gave me the courage to face my obstacles head-on.

Enrolling in a Ph.D. program was frightening, but to get where I was destined to be I had to do it. (Law school was what my mother prayed for, but that was not where I was needed.) Prayer was part of my everyday ritual. Morning, noon and evening, I prayed for God to show me what was next.

A lot happened in my life while I was in the Ph.D. program. Friends were removed, my marriage suffered and distance grew within my family. This was painful, but I came to understand that these losses were simply signs God put in place to let us know He has something better for us. For Him to pour blessings into our lives, sometimes He has to first create some space.

There's a level of understanding that goes along with faith. We have to know when to let go!

Oftentimes, when something is being removed we immediately try to hold onto it. God has something better, but we don't see this in the beginning. We have this mind-set of, "No, I don't want to let it go."

As you travel along the road of life, there will always be some people who can't get there with you. That's hard to accept, and you might even fight desperately to bring them along with you, to cling to the very people who are holding you back. But you must understand that if you continue holding on, you won't be able to open your arms and receive the blessing God has for you. You need to trust in Him, and let good things happen.

Time after time, I went through this phase of losing people who I thought would be with me throughout my journey. It wasn't necessarily part of my choice, but it was warranted. If you're destined for greatness, God will remove what is not for you and bring forward what is. Prayer will reveal what we don't know. That's when you're free to savor the blessing.

And you know what? As hard as it was, I haven't regretted losing anyone during that period. Yes, it was both tumultuous and scary. It was trying. Most of the time, I had to trust my instincts. You may feel confused and not be fully sure what's happening but know there is a reason behind it and you just have to go through. The Bible talks about going through a furnace. That's how it was for me, and that's probably how it will be for you.

Now that I know where I am, I realize being forced to let them go was a pure blessing. This doesn't mean you have to give up all of your friends or family members. It just means you need to develop the ability to recognize those that are doing ugly things behind your back, sabotaging you or impeding your progress through jealousy, resentment or even misplaced feelings of love. If only I had known then what I know now, they would have been gone in a second....

Remember God is elevating you and you're doing bigger and better things. The only people you need in your life beside family are true friends who will applaud what you're doing and support you.

Looking back on my teenage pregnancies and my abusive marriage, I understand sometimes you have to go through hell to appreciate the beautiful things – even if you don't realize those hard times are a test. When you get to the other end, you will no longer take for granted blessings that are being poured upon you.

During the hard times, my focus was only on the superficial. I was thinking, *as long as I look good to outsiders, everything is fine.* But behind closed doors, my life was a mess.

The funny part in all of this was I was so focused on my marital problems and what I saw as my husband having problems with me that it took a long time for me to recognize it was really the hand of God working in my life.

I continued attending the same church as my husband, and the pastor encouraged me to stay. *Give him time,* he said, and *he will get better.* My mind was telling me, no*, he isn't going to get better.* I was in my Ph.D. program by then, so I was able to see things more clearly.

I remember sitting in my living room working on a research paper for my Comprehensive examination, a twenty-five-page paper that I needed to deliver in two weeks. My youngest son came to me and said, "If nobody else loves you, I do".

This wonderful, loving statement from a young child opened my eyes. It was a promise that my life was about to take another major step forward. I began to look over my life and see it for what it was: *messy!*

I began to pray, to ask God to cover me. I trusted Him that I was making a sound decision in leaving, and now I can see that ending my first marriage was His way of preparing me for everything that was to come.

Those that were in our circle attempted to help me and the children as much as possible. Some of our friends, other married couples, talked to us; the men would communicate with my husband and the women with me. It didn't make me feel better. It was obvious the end was near. My thoughts turned to: *why me?* I began to pray and asked for my faith to be strengthened to carry me through.

I took a faith walk. I didn't know exactly how my spiritual and material needs would be met, but I trusted that they would be. And they were! Nevertheless, it was a testing time. My youngest daughter and son were having problems in school, and I had no money as everything I had was depleted when I left my marriage. I moved away from my hometown into an apartment that had no furniture for almost a year. My grandfather was old school, a traditionalist who didn't believe in divorce. My relationship with my family became strained, as they couldn't understand what I was going through.

But I put down roots and became part of the new community I'd moved to. I developed rich friendships that are still fruitful today. I'm close to and loved by supportive people I know I can count on in any situation. I have "sisters" and "brothers" that I can go to when I need something.

Looking back, it's clear that ending my flawed marriage was the best step I could have taken to drastically improve my life and the lives of my children.   This doesn't mean I regret my marriage, as crazy as it was, because out of it came our last son. I sacrificed a lot for my four children, under the belief that my being married would provide for them the stability and closeness I never had. I wanted them to grow into productive members of society. But even though the marriage didn't work out, all four of my wonderful children are happy, stable and productive citizens, which I count as a victory for me and the fruits of my faith.

That faith has brought me to a point where I want for nothing. Everything just comes naturally to me, and it can for you, too. To truly know God, and what He can do for you, to see how things can just flow, all you have to do is trust and have faith. I believe that faith like a mustard seed can move mountains, because that is what is happening in my life.

The minute I turned it over to God and walked by faith, things became effortless. This is why I believe all things that are good come to you when the time is right. For example, despite all of the turmoil taking place in my life at the time, the I passed my Comprehensive exams on the first try!

Since then I've opened my own consultancy, and I taught at a college and also maintained a forty-hour-per-week job. To be able to manage everything I had going on took strength that only God could provide.

I am now Dr. Nicole Sherrill-Corry! *Yay!* I own a successful mental health agency that is expanding. Some may not like it, but… oh well.

I took the hand that was dealt to me and played it to the best of my ability. And I stand firm in the belief that as long as I have God in my life and my faith remains strong, nothing is impossible.

And you can do it, too, regardless of your circumstances. You may have to go through the fire, just as the Bible says, but as long as you have God your life will be beautiful.

PLANTING SEEDS – GIVING AND RECEIVING

To further explain the concept of faith rendering results, let's discuss the principle of giving and receiving. We should view our time, money, gifts and talents as seeds. When we sow a seed, we expect that seed to take root in the ground and draw nutrients from the soil to produce a plant. This occurs only if the soil is cultivated. Likewise, we should sow our resources into good ground and expect good results. The harvest we sow is the same measure that we reap... but the measure is always more. The laws of the universe state that our harvest is always multiplied. The good we do come back to us multiplied – as does the bad. So, what's it to be?

What do I mean by sowing into good ground? I mean we need to recognize the best opportunities for doing the most good. For example, with my non-profit Women Embracing Excellence, we give scholarships to women we believe show potential to make the best of themselves through more education. Our hope is that they, in turn, will be better positioned to care for their families and pass the benefits of greater security and self-sufficiency to their children. If these women are successful, eventually we'll all reap the benefits because more stable families lead to more stable communities. And you know what else, when you help and bless others you also get to enjoy that wonderful, warm feeling that comes with ensuring another person makes something of her life.

What many don't like about this notion of faith is the fact that what happens in our life comes back full circle. It's no longer God's fault or will, but instead we become accountable for the outcomes of our choices. In having faith, we must have belief in ourselves and trust that we'll make the right choice or decision. How do we guarantee that? Well, I'm sorry to say, there are no guarantees, but there are opportunities to learn from our mistakes. Albert Einstein once said, "The definition of insanity is doing the same thing over and over again and expecting different results." When we learn from our mistakes, we avoid repeating them and going down the same road again.

We all have different learning curves, and some of us don't get it the first time. Although it takes some of us longer than others to learn from life's lessons, the most important thing is that we *do* learn. Eventually, we'll grow tired of driving around in circles and we'll equip ourselves with what we need to be successful on this road trip called life.

Dear Reader,

Like everyone else, I've lived a life filled with valleys and shadows, summits and sunshine. I learned some hard lessons, discovered my true value and have overcome.

And now, as I stand in the space God carved out for me even before I was born, looking eagerly forward to the many wonders and triumphs He still has in store for me, I thank Him for the opportunity to share my experiences with you.

I truly believe our lives are best lived in the service of others, and that even our darkest hours begin to shine bright when we use the lessons we've learned to teach, encourage and guide others.

So, with the deepest humility and greatest optimism I offer to you this book, *Advice from a Friend.* I offer it with the expectation you'll find something that encourages you while providing hope when you need it and clarity when you seek it. Likewise, I truly pray this book serves as a catalyst for you to recognize, accept and embrace <u>The Importance of You</u>.

Walk in faith, knowing that I am walking beside you holding your hand.

Yours in friendship and love,

Dr. Nicole

www.ingramcontent.com/pod-product-compliance
Lightning Source LLC
Chambersburg PA
CBHW051841090426
42736CB00011B/1918